Breaking Through the Barrier of Time

Tales of Those Who Have Entertained Visions, Visionaries, and Visitors from the Future

Conrad Bauer

ISBN: 9781728764160

Printed in the United States

Contents

Contents

The Ticking of the Clock

Time. The innocuous ticking of the clock is a constant reminder of how quickly it passes, and most of us can't seem to find enough of it. We try our best to squeeze more hours out of a 24-hour day, but we remain forever fixed within those finite parameters. But what if there was a way to free ourselves from the bounds of time? What if there was a way to move beyond the strict confines of the clock and experience past and future realities at will?

The concept of time travel is always going to be a controversial one. Critics insist that it is fraught with paradoxes and inconsistencies. And perhaps they're right. But even if time travel is impossible, what about seeing into the future? There have been prophets, seers, and visionaries all over the world who have claimed such clairvoyance for centuries. Were they all elaborate frauds?

In this book we will examine the veracity of such claims as we tell the tales of those who have supposedly entertained visions, visionaries, even visitors from the future. So, whether you are a true believer or a skeptic at heart, withhold your judgment for a moment as we escape the incessant ticking of the clock to look back at those who say they've looked far, far forward.

Visions of the Future Perceived in the Past

Since history has been recorded, it has recorded accounts of prophets and prophecies. From the oracles of ancient Greece to the acclaimed Renaissance prophet Nostradamus, there has been a long line of supposed seers who have posited unique visions of the future.

Some proved to be completely off-base in their predictions, but others prophesied with surprising accuracy. In this chapter we will go down the long and eclectic list of visionaries and soothsayers who in the distant past attempted to stake their own claims on the future.

Cassandra—Fate's Cruel Mistress

In the world of ancient Greece, the line between mythology and reality was often blurred—so much so that it is sometimes hard to ascertain whether certain people and places ever really existed. The city of Knossos on the island of Crete, for example, was long thought to be purely mythical—just a made-up locale for Greek storytelling—until its ruins were discovered by archeologists in the early 20th century. Then again, you have Herodotus, the so-called "father of history", who made it a point to give historical figures impossible—and completely fictional—traits.

It was in this strange epoch of time, right on the nubilous edge of a recorded history hopelessly mixed with myth, that one of the oldest clairvoyants on record resided. Cassandra's story, which the modern mind cannot help but categorize as legend, may well have been taken as gospel truth by her contemporaries.

The narrative stars one of the capricious Greek gods, Apollo, who fell in love with the mortal woman and granted her incredible prophetic abilities to win her affection. After being endowed with the gift of foresight, however, Cassandra apparently saw what lay in store for her and did not care for it one whit. Repulsed by the vision of being caught in Apollo's clutches, she firmly refused the deity's further advances. The spurned god responded by mumbling a few arcane words that affixed a curse onto the comely clairvoyant: Even though her visions of the future would remain true, from that day forward no one would believe her. She would come to warn her fellow citizens of impending war and the fall of Troy, but no one heeded her. The city was sacked and Cassandra herself was raped, enslaved, and ultimately murdered.

It's a grim note on which to begin, but fortunately enough, the rest of the seers in this chapter found a more receptive audience and a happier fate.

Saint Malachy and the Prophecies of Fatima

Before being canonized in 1190, Saint Malachy was a simple Irish monk by the name of Malachy O'Morgair. Malachy was born in Armagh in 1094 and supposedly received an Earth-shattering vision of the future in 1139 while in Rome on a pilgrimage to the Vatican. The revelation took the form of a "papal roster" revealing all the popes from his time until the end of the world. Malachy wrote down brief descriptive commentaries on each of these popes and handed them to Pope Innocent II for safekeeping.

If the legend is to be believed, this document then stayed hidden in the Vatican archives for about 400 years—until a Benedictine monk by the name of Dom Arnold de Wyon just happened upon the manuscript while doing research in the Vatican's giant library. Many have since pounced on de Wyon's claim that he suddenly discovered the Malachy manuscripts 400 years after the fact. For skeptics, this is a red flag suggesting that the whole thing was fabricated by de Wyon himself.

But while the 400-year gap between the document's alleged provenance and its discovery is indeed suspicious, what lends credence to the Malachy claim is the prophecies themselves. So far they have seemed fairly on-target in their portrayal of the papal line. One entry, for example, seems to deftly describe the only Briton to attain the papacy. Saint Malachy's commentary for the slot that was ultimately filled by British Pope Adrian IV described him as "*De rure Albo*", which means "from the Alban country". The word "Alban" is derived from the old Roman name for Britain, "Albion".

Another seemingly fitting appellation is given for the reign of Pope Benedict XV, who presided over the Vatican from 1914 to 1922. Malachy's prophetic designation for this pope was "*Religio Depopulata*", literally meaning "Religion Depopulated". This at first glance might seem like an odd phrase to be associated with the leader of the largest religious denomination in the world, but it begins to make sense when you consider the events that occurred between 1914 and 1922. Religion was indeed depopulated during this period, for a few reasons. First, through sheer loss of life. World War I occurred during these years, after all, and significantly depopulated much of Europe, leading to a decline in the numbers of Christian faithful simply through casualties of war. Second, following the Russian Revolution of 1917, Communist ideologues in that country sought to shut down the Russian Church, persecuting and killing countless Christians in the process. Last but not least, Charles Darwin's theory of evolution sparked a major shift in intellectual thought in the United States, causing many Americans to fall away from the faith. (Yes, it is true that Darwin first proposed his theory back in 1859. But in America, it wasn't until the early 1920s that evolution gained widespread acceptance and Darwin's teachings began to be included in school curricula.) So, taking all this into account, ascribing "Religion Depopulated" to the pope who reigned during these contentious years really does seem nothing short of prophetic.

His successor, Pope Pius XI, had an even harder time of it. Given by Malachy the prophetic marker "Unshaken Faith", Pius XI found himself surrounded by the fascist governments of Spain, Italy, and Germany. He *had* to have unshaken faith in order to navigate through these turbulent waters. Although he has come in for much criticism recently, with some of his most outspoken critics calling him nothing short of a fascist collaborator, the reality is that Pope Pius XI stood up to both Hitler and Mussolini at a time when most stayed silent. In 1938, for example, when Mussolini signed an agreement with Hitler to start enforcing anti-Semitic laws in Italy, the Pope immediately denounced the Italian dictator and declared that Christians and Jews were brothers of kindred faiths, and that Christians by nature were "spiritually Semites" themselves. The next year he gave a speech boldly condemning Nazism as "fundamentally racist and anti-Christian."

From the safety of today, some scoff at such remarks as being too little too late, but the fact is that they could easily have led Pius XI to the gas chamber. In the end, Pope Pius XI proved himself a man of unshaken faith just as Malachy described. At the risk of his own life, he emphatically told the dictators who were oppressing Europe that he would not bend, he would not budge, he would not compromise his faith for their evil agenda.

It's hard to know what retribution the fascists may have been planning for this outspoken pope, since he passed away of natural causes (as far as we know) shortly thereafter in 1939. But it is said that he had managed to irk Mussolini so much that upon receiving word of this pope's demise, the Italian dictator shouted in relief, "At last, that stubborn old man is dead!" Mussolini may have named Pius XI "stubborn", but Malachy named him first: "unshaken". If your faith is unshaken enough to ruffle the feathers of a blowhard tyrant like Mussolini, you know you must be doing something right!

The next pope and also the next Pius—Pius XII—was notated by Malachy as "Angelic Shepherd". It was up to him to shepherd his flock through the worst of World War Two and its aftermath, so once again, it would seem that Malachy was on target.

John Paul II was another Pope whose Malachy classification at first seemed odd but would later prove fitting. Reigning from 1978 until his death in 2005, John Paul II was one of the most popular popes of all time. But all Malachy had to say about him was "*De Medietate Lunae*"—"The Labor of the Sun". Seems like utter nonsense, right? Well, coincidentally or not, John Paul II had the strange honor of having both his birth and death occur during a solar eclipse! The odds of being treated to an eclipse of the sun on both the day you are born and the day you die are—no pun intended—simply astronomical.

There is much conjecture about Malachy's papal prophecies—whether they are true and what they might mean. But for those who believe them, one thing is certain: The papal line is soon coming to an end. Malachy predicted that there would only be 112 popes, with the last pope serving his tenure during a cataclysmic destruction of Rome. Pope John Paul II was the 110th pope, which made his successor Pope Benedict XVI the 111th. Now that Benedict XVI has been succeeded by Pope

Francis, some have naturally claimed that Francis is then the final 112th Pope. But there are others who argue that since Benedict resigned and is still alive, we are still in the 111th pope era with Francis as just a temporary fill-in until the real 112th pope emerges after Benedict's death.

But whoever the 112th pope might be, the prognosis—the only one of any substantial length that Malachy gave—does not sound good. In regard to this final pope, Malachy warns us, "In the extreme persecution of the Holy Roman Church, there will sit Peter the Roman, who will pasture his sheep in many tribulations; and when these things are finished, the city of seven hills will be destroyed, and the terrible judge will judge his people. The End." Yes, like some sadistic uncle telling the scariest bedtime story ever, Malachy prophesies that the Catholic Church will face many struggles and persecutions as the last pope leads it through the chaos—until it's all over and we reach—"The End".

Speaking of the city of the seven hills—Rome—being destroyed, Malachy's prophecy envisions complete and utter annihilation of the Vatican. Interestingly, three schoolchildren from Fatima, Portugal, had a very similar vision of the future of the Church nearly 800 years later. In the early 20th century, these children claimed that the Virgin Mary appeared to them and showed them scenes from the last days. In them, they saw a pope—apparently the *last* pope—walking through the rubble of a city that had been flattened by a horrendous war. The pope seemed to be looking for survivors as he walked "trembling, with halting step" through the wreckage, but in the end all this sad figure could do was pray for the souls of the corpses he met on his way.

The Fatima kids then saw this future pope climb a big hill crowned with a rough-hewn cross. He dropped to his knees in prayer in front of this cross—and then several soldiers rushed toward him, opening fire and shot him dead with rapid bursts of their machine guns. Was this martyred pope that these children observed in their vision the same 112th, final Pope that Malachy spoke of? Time will tell—and it will not be much time.

Michel Nostradamus

NOSTRADAMUS

Perhaps no prophet has captured the world's attention like the man known to us as Nostradamus. Born in the sleepy French village of St. Remy de Provence on December 14, 1503, Nostradamus started his professional life not as a prophet but as a physician. In this vocation he gained early fame simply by surviving several years of direct contact with the plague victims he treated. When so many others died from such contact, might it be that that someone was looking out for Nostradamus, perhaps saving him for some greater purpose in life? But whether or not that's the case, it was during his clinical practice that Nostradamus began to have visionary experiences—and his predictions would soon come to shock the world with their accuracy. Nearly 500 years later, the world is still completely mesmerized by his prophecies.

Part of the enchantment stems from the way Nostradamus wrote them down. Instead of just laying everything out in plain English—or in Nostradamus's case, plain Middle French—he wrote his words of wisdom out in word puzzles called "quatrains". The enigmatic nature of his artful riddles has enticed many to try to solve them.

Of course, as Nostradamus's critics are quick to point out, the vague, airy nature of these pieces of prophetic prose allows us to arrive at almost *any* solution after the fact. It is in fact rather easy, after some earthshaking event, to flip through Nostradamus's writings and find a quatrain that seems to describe exactly what happened. It sometimes seems that just about anything could happen, and with a little effort you could find a quatrain to match it.

But not all of Nostradamus's prophecies are so easily dismissed as mere fanciful retrospection. There are certain claims that cannot be immediately discounted as wishful thinking. Take, for example, one of his very first predictions, which he made on a trip to Italy during which he became acquainted with a few Franciscan monks. Nostradamus identified one of the monks, a man named Felice Peretti, as a future pope—and Peretti indeed ascended to the Throne of Saint Peter as Pope Sixtus V in 1585, several years after Nostradamus passed away.

After Nostradamus returned to France, he began to pursue his visionary experiences full-time. He would close himself up in a room late at night and stare into a bowl of water filled with aromatic herbs. As he breathed in their fragrance he would enter a trance-like state in which he saw visions of the future. And to his credit, most of the things that he prophesied would happen during his own lifetime did indeed occur.

For example, Nostradamus made a prediction in regard to the King of France stating that “a young lion would overcome an older one on the field of battle”. He would “pierce his eyes through a golden cage” and the old king would then “die a cruel death.” Nostradamus went straight to the king to warn him that this prophecy was indeed about him and that he should avoid jousting at all costs. Understandably, the incredulous king simply ignored the strange, monkish Nostradamus. He had cause to regret it a few years later, however, when he engaged in a jousting match with a younger man. The match ended with a lance piercing the king’s golden visor and his eye, inflicting a fatal brain injury. The wounded king lingered on in excruciating pain for another week before succumbing to the blow dealt him by the “young lion”.

Nostradamus is also said to have predicted the date of his own death, as well as the date that grave robbers would break into his tomb—a prophecy verified by a medallion the robbers found inscribed with the exact date of their crime. This is all well and good, of course, but what does it have to say about the far future—i.e., our present? Just what did Nostradamus predict about our own times, and what lies ahead of them?

Well, some say that Nostradamus predicted ongoing global war on terror—which was allegedly kicked off by one of the few quatrains Nostradamus tagged with an exact date. That date was 1999, and the quatrain read, “In the seventh month of 1999, a great king of terror will descend on the world." Of course, the ninth month of 2001 might make more sense than the seventh month of 1999 in this context; it was on September 11, 2001, after all, that a great king of terror descended in the form of hijacked planes crashing into the World Trade Center, the Pentagon and a Pennsylvania field. Still, we might allow the man a *small* margin of error after nearly 500 years, and some explain the discrepancy by claiming that the events that led up to 9/11 actually did begin in July of 1999.

Basically, Nostradamus predicted that World War III would start in 1999 and last for 27 years. If you view the war on terror as an unsung World War III, that means that we can expect it to wrap up sometime in 2026. The manner in which this will supposedly happen, however, is somewhat surprising. According to Nostradamus, "France will be assaulted by five countries through neglect. Tunis, Algiers—stirred up by the Persians (Iranians). Leon, Seville and Barcelona will fail. They will not have the fleet because of the Venetians." With unusual specificity, Nostradamus seems to be foretelling a surprise attack involving the countries of Tunisia and Algeria, led by Iran, which delivers a devastating blow to France while conquering parts of Spain.

Now, let's consider this as an allegory derived from Nostradamus's viewpoint as a man of the 16th century. The Venetians were the leading maritime power of the day, so the reference to Venice can be taken to mean Europe's naval strength as a whole. Thus, Nostradamus is predicting that a gap in the continent's Mediterranean defenses will allow a massive Islamic army to break through and lay waste to France while actually holding territory in Spain.

But as dire as that sounds, take heart—Nostradamus gives us a little more time than Saint Malachy. In fact, he doesn't actually predict the end of the world until 3797! And what's more, in his cryptic writing he seems to allude to space travel and the migration of humanity to other star systems to escape whatever calamity has befallen Earth. As Nostradamus explains in a quatrain for that year, “The world will be approaching a great conflagration—some will assemble in Aquarius for several years, others in Cancer for a longer time.” To some, the only possible interpretation is that Nostradamus was referencing a future interstellar colonization of far-flung solar systems inside these two constellations.

So, if we are to believe the prophetic words of Michel Nostradamus, despite all of the turmoil, strife, and chaos, we can still hold our heads high. Because humanity’s fate still lies somewhere in the stars.

Edgar Cayce

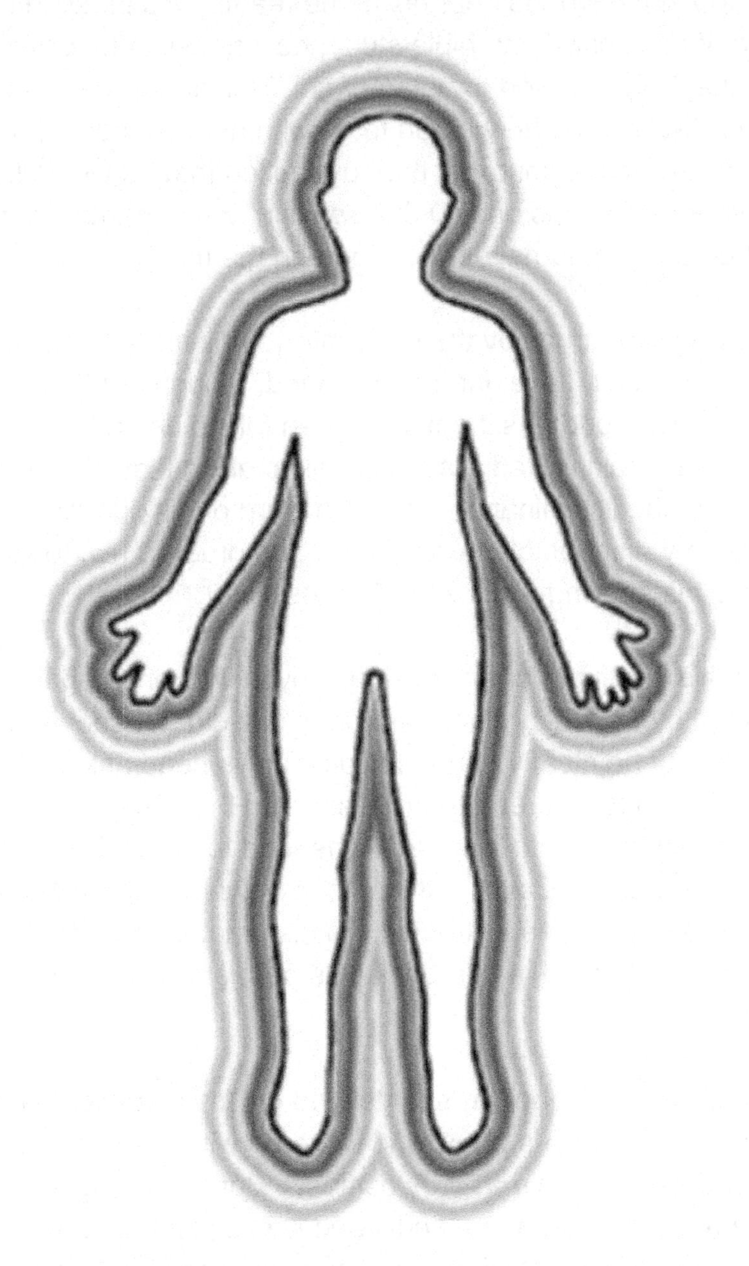

Edgar Cayce was born the son of a simple Kentucky farmer in 1877, and he was expected to follow in his family's rather unremarkable footsteps. But this was not meant to be. Cayce later recalled that his first indication that he was meant for a higher purpose came when he was 12 years old, spending a lazy afternoon in the woods near his home reading his bible. In the middle of this impromptu bible study, he was beset by a winged figure that he perceived to be an angel. This figure asked the terrified Cayce what he wanted to do with his life "most of all". Summoning up his courage, the boy replied that he would like to help others. After this brief Q & A session, the apparition simply vanished as if it had never been there in the first place.

Cayce was awestruck by the encounter, but initially decided to keep it to himself. It weighed on his mind, though, and back in the mundane world of school, he began falling behind his classmates, making bad grades on his spelling tests. When his father, a strict disciplinarian, received word of his dismal scores, he was very disappointed with Cayce and ordered him to stay up studying his spelling—all night, if necessary.

During this late-night cram session, Cayce was once again contacted by the entity from the woods. He did not see the being this time, but he clearly heard its voice in his head asking him to listen. The celestial creature promised him that if he would simply sleep, he would learn all he needed to know. Probably glad of the excuse, Cayce put his head down on his textbook and took a nap just as instructed. To his amazement, when he woke up, every word in that book was permanently ingrained in his brain.

It must be every schoolboy's fantasy to lay his head down on a textbook as if it were a pillow and wake up with the contents absorbed into his brain as if by osmosis. But according to Cayce, this is precisely what happened—and it was just the very beginning of a long life of extraordinary clairvoyant perception, almost all of it occurring while he slept!

This perception soon encompassed future events as well as spelling lists, and it's little wonder that Cayce became known as "The Sleeping Prophet". Talking in his sleep, he successfully predicted events regarding World War Two and the deaths of FDR and JFK, just to name a few. He also proved able to diagnose any illness and prescribe treatment to cure it.

Despite the power of his abilities, as a young man Cayce was initially hesitant to embrace them, worrying that they went against mainstream Christian teachings. But by the early 1900s he had come to accept his unusual gifts and managed to reconcile them with his still-strong faith in Christ—even when he began to believe in the possibility of reincarnation of the human soul. This belief was based on his personal experience of several of his own past lives and those of others—as well as one of his *future* lives!

Yes, in one of Cayce's most sensational sleep sessions ever, he supposedly found himself projected into a future life that he will live around the year 2100. He experienced the world of the future as a young man living with his parents in a residential community somewhere in Nebraska. But the world of 2100 was a lot different from what Cayce knew, or what we know—although in an era of concern about climate change, it seems like a terrifyingly plausible prediction. According to Edgar Cayce, during this epoch the world had just passed through great environmental changes, and since the West Coast had sunk under the sea, Nebraska was now on the coastline of a much-diminished United States.

When the future Cayce explained to his parents that his spirit was visiting from the past, they took him to see a group of reincarnation specialists—a cadre of future scientists who apparently knew all about this sort of thing—and they vigorously sought to uncover the traces of his old life. As far-fetched as it may seem, these researchers not only believed his story, they took such an avid interest in it that they booked him a flight onboard a cigar-shaped metal craft (a bit reminiscent of many of the UFO sightings that would being occurring after Cayce's death) to retrace the steps of his past.

In this vehicle, Cayce toured his old stomping grounds of Ohio, Michigan, Kentucky, Alabama, and Virginia, which were almost completely underwater. They also hovered over New York City, where Cayce had briefly lived and worked, and he was amazed to see that it was mostly destroyed as well. However, work crews were attempting to rebuild the city. According to Cayce, although the denizens of this future world obviously had advanced technology and great intellect and understanding, cooperation was extremely lacking. As such it was very hard to get industry mobilized for major projects, and it was for this reason that large-scale efforts such as resurrecting the devastated skyline of New York City had been delayed for so long.

It may not be the future that we would like to envision, but Cayce believed it to be true, and if anyone begged to differ, the Sleeping Prophet would merely suggest that they—"sleep on it".

Baba Vanga

She was known to many as the Bulgarian Nostradamus. Her predictions have shocked the world with both their far-reaching scope and their immediate accuracy. But just who was the prophetess Baba Vanga? She was born Vangeliya Dimitrova in 1911 in what was then the backwater outskirts of the Ottoman Empire. At the time of her birth, that empire—long known as the "sick man of Europe"—was indeed on its last legs. It broke apart just a few years later during the turmoil of World War I, and the land of her birth briefly became part of Bulgaria, the nation that would claim her as its own for the rest of her life.

Baba Vanga grew up poor, but aside from this she had a fairly normal life until fate intervened when she was 12 years old. During a bad storm, a tornado literally picked her off the ground and carried her several feet before throwing her down again. She was injured in the fall, but the worst part was that her eyes were completely filled with sand and dust. Her body recovered from this freak accident, but her eyes did not. She slowly lost the ability to see and eventually went blind.

But even as her two physical eyes closed for good, her "third eye", the eye of extrasensory perception, opened wide. By the time of World War II she had become widely known for the predictions that she made, and during the course of the conflict many people consulted her to learn the fate of family members who were missing in action. And at one point even Bulgarian Tsar Boris III sought audience with Baba Vanga.

The notoriety of this Nostradamus of the East continued to grow over the next decades as Baba Vanga continued to make startlingly accurate predictions both about the lives of individuals and about world events. One of her biggest predictions was that the Soviet Union would collapse, which duly occurred in 1991. Baba Vanga died after this prophecy was fulfilled, at the age of 85. Before her death, however, she left the world with a series of prophecies recorded for posterity. Some of them are said to have already transpired, but many more have yet to be fulfilled.

Among the most hyped of her posthumous prophecies is the one said to have predicted the 9/11 terrorist attacks on the United States: "Horror! Horror! The American brethren will fall after being attacked by the steel birds!" Although this statement is admittedly vague, it's not that much of a stretch to link the American "brethren" to the "twin" towers in New York and the "steel birds" to the hijacked airplanes that brought them down.

Some of Baba Vanga's visions of what still lay in store were much more direct, however—such as her prophecy of an "Islamic State" arising in Syria around the year 2010 and leading to destabilization and massive migration of Muslims to Europe. The authenticity of this prediction has been hotly debated, but if she actually made it, it's hard to avoid the conclusion that the current conflict with ISIS is precisely what Baba Vanga was referring to.

On the other hand, Baba Vanga also seems to have made one clearly failed prophecy about recent events: She predicted that the 44th President of the United States, who turned out to be Barack Obama, would be the *last* President of the United States. Following the inauguration of Donald Trump as the 45th president, this is obviously not the case—at least in the literal sense. There are some true believers who argue that the decidedly unconventional Trump has vitiated the norms and standards of presidential leadership to such an extent that the presidency really did end with Obama!

They can point to the massive number of protesters who took to the streets for the "Not My President's Day March" shortly after Trump took office. And there certainly is a growing chorus claiming that Trump has singlehandedly "destroyed the office of the presidency". Was this rejection of number 45 by a large segment of society what Baba Vanga was referring to? At any rate, it has given her supporters grounds for maintaining that even with this prediction, their favorite prophetess was really not that far off the mark.

However you feel about Trump and the survival of the U.S. presidency as an institution, you'll probably be happy to hear Baba Vanga's next prophecy: She predicted that some near-future government will make great technological strides and actually find means of stamping out world hunger for good by 2025. It's not clear whether this will be accomplished through mass produced genetically modified superfoods or some other innovation, but according to Baba Vanga, food will soon be a commodity that everyone will have easy access to.

And there's more good news ahead. In one of her more unusual predictions, Baba Vanga also prophesied that just a few years after the eradication of hunger an unspecified nation will send an expedition to Venus to exploit an exotic new energy source. The obvious problem is that, according to current scientific understanding, such a mission would be impossible since Venus is far too hot for a manned landing. Only a few unmanned spacecraft have managed to land on the planet, and they have only managed to snap off a few photos before they were destroyed—melted after just a few seconds of exposure to the blast furnace environment of this hellish world. Of course, the inhospitable nature of Venus was already well known when Baba Vanga made this prediction in the early 1990s, so perhaps she also perceived some development that would make the expedition possible—either a technological advance or a change in the Venusian climate.

Speaking of climate change, though, takes us back to Earth and to Baba Vanga's next, much less pleasant prediction: A buildup of greenhouse gases will cause our planet's polar ice caps to melt completely by 2033, leading to cataclysmic flooding worldwide.

For the 2040s, Baba Vanga foretold a stunning development in the global war on terror in which Rome falls to Muslim armies. Whether not you believe in this particular prophetess, it's certainly interesting to note that she's not the only one to have predicted the destruction of Rome by a foreign army around this time. The children of Fatima did, Nostradamus did, and so did Saint Malachy before him with his famous vision of the last pope presiding over a bombed out Rome just before "The End". Baba Vanga's prophecy, though, is both less final and less tragic: According to her, the Muslim conquerors, after the initial devastation, eventually prove themselves to be good stewards, and the European economy actually improves under their reign.

Meanwhile, the United States remains a force to be reckoned with and continues to make steady advances in technology. Innovations in medicine, for example, will make it possible to reproduce all bodily organs. And unlike the Venusian expedition, recent discoveries in stem cell research make such a development seem highly plausible. Stem cells, you see, are cells found in the human embryo which have the capacity to become any cell of the body. You can take a stem cell and coax it into becoming a lung cell, a heart cell, etc. This has already led to the regrowth of vital tissues from these cells, and yes, it is believed that someday whole organs could possibly be grown this way as well. These are fairly recent developments in medicine—some of the biggest breakthroughs occurred between 2006 and 2010—and so it's quite impressive that a blind and illiterate woman living in a small village in Bulgaria back in the early 1990s would have known that such things would be possible.

According to Baba Vanga, the U.S. will continue to make progress in many fields besides medicine, and will eventually turn its research towards military technology with the aim of reasserting its global hegemony. This second Manhattan Project culminates in the year 2066, when a resurgent America launches a secret "weather weapon" against Muslim-occupied Rome. Having learned how to manipulate local weather conditions, the

U.S. is able to send lightning bolts and torrents of hail down upon their enemies in the Roman Caliphate, and this futuristic version of "shock and awe" finally settles the score and ends the long global war on terror. Baba Vanga foresaw no more big wars after this, only a skirmish between small countries breaking out in 2123 while the big countries stay out of it.

Shortly after this, things get interesting once again when a research station in Hungary picks up a signal from ET in the year 2125. These aliens then pay the Earth a personal visit in 2130. They turn out to be water dwellers, and they show their new human friends how to build cities under the oceans. Even as people begin to colonize the seafloor, space colonization also picks up pace, and by 2183 a colony on Mars is so advanced that it declares independence. Humanity becomes a divided species, residing on two separate planets with two distinct cultures.

But exploring the unknown frontier of space is not all fun and games. Following further forays into the search for extraterrestrial life, humanity will stumble upon something "truly terrible" in the year 2221. Whether this is a completely hostile and malevolent group of aliens or some other unforeseen deep space danger, Baba Vanga never fully elaborated. But on a positive note, whatever we might face, we will face it together. By this point, Baba Vanga predicted, humanity will have forgotten all about petty squabbles of the past and will be more united than ever before. This universal spirit of cooperation will even lead to the discovery of a limited form of time travel in the year 2288!

As interesting as all these claims are, you have to ask yourself—are these strange musings really a portrait of the future? Or was Baba Vanga's true gift simply for storytelling? Well—I suppose only time will time.

Remote Viewers
An Alleged Timeline of the Future

The extrasensory phenomenon known as remote viewing certainly existed long before famed psychic guru Ingo Swann coined the term back in the early 1970s, but it wasn't until the U.S. government began to take an interest that the classification really took hold. The U.S. military first became interested in remote viewing research when American spies snooping on the Soviet Union reported that the Russians were utilizing a new cadre of psychic warriors trained to use their minds to locate hidden military targets.

Now, during the Cold War, the American government had a world-class case of "keeping up with the Joneses". Often enough, hearing that their arch rivals the Soviets were involved in a particular area of research was all it took for the U.S. to jump in with both feet. And so, hot on the heels of the highly competitive space race of the previous decade, the psychotronic race for clairvoyant capability got underway.

The U.S. military's first official remote viewing work took place in Menlo Park, California, in 1972. Famed adepts such as Uri Geller, the Israeli known for bending spoons with his mind, as well as Ingo Swann himself, were heavily involved from the start. However, it was Geller who seems to have set the stage for just how the experiments would be carried out.

Geller was already a well-known celebrity due to the "stage magic" and mentalist-type feats he had used to woo crowds in his native Israel, the United States and elsewhere before becoming involved with the program. His involvement began when he was detained by the CIA for questioning in August of 1973. The agents placed the psychic in an isolated room and began to poke and prod him in an attempt to ascertain the scope of his supposed extrasensory abilities. The initial tests were quite simple: An operative in another room in the building would draw a picture, and Geller was given a sheet of paper and a writing utensil and asked to reproduce the image. There was no way that Geller could have seen what this other individual had drawn except through a psychic talent for remote viewing.

This was apparently the CIA's litmus test for starting a research program dedicated to this unknown and previously untested phenomenon. The path forward hinged on Geller's results—and the early proponents of the program would not be disappointed. With incredible accuracy, Geller rattled off drawing after drawing that almost perfectly matched what the isolated artist had come up with.

After this successful trial run, the Stargate remote viewing program began in earnest. At first the remote viewers were simply used to visualize faraway targets such as military headquarters, weapon supply depots and the like. But a few years into the program, it was discovered that some remote viewers seemed to have the capacity to project their minds into the future to visualize future events as well as remote locales.

This remains among the most controversial aspects of a controversial program, with some of those involved claiming that these attempts at prophecy were an absolute success and skeptics claiming that they were an absolute failure. But just what did this project, which was funded for over two decades at a cost of over 20 million dollars, find out about our future? Here is a future timeline, starting with the year 2020, of the Stargate remote viewers' most sensational findings.

2020

Government guidelines for the provision of medical services will be established. Assisted suicide will be legal and even common.

The ongoing debate about Obamacare has indeed featured warnings of a future of heavily rationed medical treatment. And while we're not quite there yet on euthanasia, remember Sarah Palin's "They're going to pull the plug on grandma"? Critics of government-run healthcare claim that euthanasia will be pushed on the terminally ill—or even the chronically sick—to reduce the strain on resources. Could this grim future come true if a democratic socialists wins the White House is 2020? We'll know in a couple of years.

2020 will bring "sufficiently hard proof" that UFOs are indeed spacecraft piloted by extraterrestrial beings.

Some UFO buffs say this means that the government will release all its secret information on ETs this year. They speculate that the Pentagon's December 2017 acknowledgement of recent UFO investigations was the beginning of a process that will culminate with a watershed moment in 2020—exactly as the remote viewers predicted.

There will be an explosion in the discovery of habitable exoplanets.

This is one Stargate prediction that's already coming true. The potential not just for life, but for widespread life throughout the cosmos, has become a very real possibility.

2025

Most people will forgo the conventional oven for complete premade meals that can be cooked in seconds.

While plausible, this is hardly earthshattering, and hardly unpredictable from the vantage point of the 1970s; it seems to be nothing more than a futuristic projection of the classic TV dinner. Let's just hope that these new-and-improved microwave meals come without the soggy mashed potatoes so common in the old ones!

Increased environmental awareness will spur efforts to reduce humanity's environmental footprint and conserve energy whenever possible. Air scrubbers will be used to improve air quality. All light bulbs will be low wattage and long-lasting.

This prediction holds an impressive amount of precognitive prescience. Air scrubbers do exist—they're filtration systems that can suck harmful toxins out of the air—and it's entirely possible that they will be in wider use by 2025. As for the ecofriendly light bulbs, just consider the LEDs that have become so prevalent over the past decade.

AI-equipped smart homes will proactively cater to our every need, monitor our vital signs, and notify authorities in an emergency. All electronic devices will be voice activated.

Smart homes are already a much-discussed concept, and it's easy to believe that they could be a lot more capable by 2025. There's also good reason to hope they will. Aside from the convenience, AI that could summon emergency medical help could save countless lives. Of course, it could also lead to some rather comic situations. Just imagine a reluctant patient arguing with his wall:

"I'm sorry, Dave, but I see that your blood pressure is rising rapidly and a heart attack is imminent. I'm going to send for an ambulance."

"Darn it! I told you, it's just indigestion! I ate some bad Taco Bell—that's all! I don't need an ambulance!"

But no matter how much Dave argues, Big Brother knows best. The paramedics are already on their way. And, of course, that brings us to the downside of such a high-tech Siri/Alexa. Once it can, AI *will* start calling the shots. Sometimes that may be a dream come true; other times it may be a headache-inducing nightmare. But either way, at the rate we're going, it does seem to be an accurate description of our future.

2030

Printed media will have disappeared completely. There will be no newspapers, no books, no magazines, not even any paper coupons. Everything will be digital.

Nowadays such a prediction seems fairly uncontroversial, even banal. With the advent of e-books and online newspapers, much of what used to be printed has indeed been digitized. If the trend continues, there really won't be much paper left by 2030. However, for the remote viewers of the 1970s, working long before the development of the World Wide Web, this on-point prediction seems to represent a very impressive instance of precognition.

Discontented voters will drift away from the traditional two-party system. There will be three mainline political parties in American: the Republicans, the Democrats, and the new American Freedom Party. Campaigning and voting will all be done online.

American politics is unquestionably in the middle of a major upheaval, so this prediction doesn't seem too far-fetched at the moment. Of course, concerns about vote fraud will have to be settled before online voting can become a reality. Perhaps by 2030 everyone will have failsafe login methods, signing on to vote with a piece of personally identifiable information that cannot be compromised.

Regulatory changes designed to curtail fraud in international money transfers will lead to the consolidation of the U.S. banking industry to just four major banks. Banks will issue loans secured by prospective organ donations.

While the first of these predictions may well be on track—both regulation and the pace of consolidation have increased somewhat in recent years—the second is nothing short of shocking. To date, there is no way to offer your kidney as collateral—but according to the remote viewers of Project Stargate, if you want a loan come 2030, you may have to pledge an organ to get it!

A new camouflage/cloaking technique utilizing an electrical current flowing over soldiers' uniforms will be able to bend light and mirror their surroundings so that they are essentially invisible to the naked eye. Sporadic fighting will have begun in a low-level World War III.

Military development of active camouflage is well underway—we can only hope that the buildup to World War III is not!

Rome will be overrun and destroyed by any Islamic army or massive numbers of refugees from the Middle East.

Well, that's interesting—once again, we're back to the destruction of Rome, as previously prophesied by the likes of Nostradamus, Saint Malachy, the children of Fatima, and the Bulgarian mystic Baba Vanga. To hear so many clairvoyants report the exact same future event is rather startling, to say the least!

2035

The Central Intelligence Agency will cease to exist.

This one must have made the remote viewers' CIA handlers cringe a bit, and some wags have suggested that perhaps it was this finding that led to the end of Project Stargate. Was the agency attempting to ensure its own survival by firing the remote viewers predicting its demise?

The first quantum computer will be rolled out.

Perhaps the Central Intelligence Agency was no longer needed because it was replaced by a massively powerful computer. Quantum computers have been the subject of intensive R&D over the past 10 years, and rudimentary prototypes have already been created. A fully functional model would have computing capacity so great that it could manage the affairs of an entire nation all by itself. The remote viewers' assertion that these incredibly advanced machines would be able to solve multistate problems which would otherwise require many man-years in just a matter of minutes is today regarded as simple fact. If such a thing can be made, it will unquestionably revolutionize almost every aspect of our lives.

The Montauk Project Inspiration for Much Stranger Things

Since the summer of 2016, sci-fi fans have been abuzz about a web series called *Stranger Things*. Set in the fictional town of Hawkins, Indiana, the series centers on a group of characters who are faced with paranormal outbursts seemingly linked to experiments conducted by the U.S. Department of Energy.

It's a great plot device, to be sure—but what many who enjoy this entertaining and well-written show are aware of is that its main themes are actually based on (allegedly) real-life events far more fantastic than anything thus far depicted in any episode of *Stranger Things*. And what was the inspiration for this popular series? A little thing called the Montauk Project.

The Mysteries of Montauk

The Montauk Project was based not in Indiana but on the East Coast, in Montauk, New York. It is here, at a little-known World War II era military installation called Camp Hero, that government scientists are said to have engaged in experiments that tampered with the very fabric of space and time.

The self-proclaimed whistle blower of this story is an electrical engineer named Preston Nichols who was hired by a Long Island defense contractor and placed on a team tasked with studying the effect of electromagnetic fields on psychically sensitive individuals. This was during the early 1970s, when the aforementioned Project Stargate was in full swing, and this has led to speculation that Nichols's work was somehow connected to these remote viewing efforts. But while Project Stargate was officially declassified in 1995, its connection to Montauk, if any, remains murky.

At any rate, Nichols began working at Montauk, and then he suddenly began to have problems. Too many of his subjects were drawing blanks and having mental blocks. He immediately suspected that some sort of outside interference was affecting the experiments. He was working with electromagnetic fields, after all, and some powerful signal from a radio tower, radar installation or the like could have been impacting the research. It didn't take him long to decide that the massive radar antenna at nearby Camp Hero was the most likely culprit. But when he called up the base to ask about it, he was given the runaround and never received an answer to his inquiries.

It was only years later, when Nichols learned that Camp Hero had been closed, that he began to do some serious detective work on his own. He arrived to find the former military installation completely abandoned. In fact, it was not only abandoned, it was shockingly disheveled. Papers were strewn everywhere, tables were overturned, and equipment had been hastily turned off, apparently in mid-run. There were signs of a disordered and hasty retreat everywhere he turned. But for what reason? This was certainly not the standard way to mothball an army base.

As he walked among the debris, he noticed several electric amplifiers lying around in the yard. Such high-tech equipment was hard to come by, and he was surprised to find it so callously discarded. But the abandoned gear would be useful for his own research into electromagnetic fields, so he got in touch with military officials to ask if he could have it. Surprisingly, he was given the green light to salvage whatever he wanted.

Nichols wasn't able to inveigle any information as to why the base had been abandoned so quickly, but he was happy to get some top-notch equipment for free. He promptly set out on his salvage mission, and while he was collecting what he'd come for, he came upon a homeless person camping out in the yard of the old base. In itself, that wasn't an unusual sight in the New York/New Jersey area, but this particular homeless man had quite a story to tell. He readily revealed what the Army hadn't and told Nichols an incredible tale about what had caused the sudden closure of Camp Hero.

According to him, physicists at the site had managed to open a portal to another world and then a monster had waltzed right through it. That already sounds like plenty of material for a Hollywood science fiction thriller, but there was another plot twist to come. Because as the vagabond continued to talk, he suddenly recognized his visitor and his eyes widened as he sputtered that Nichols was "one of them"—that is, one of the researchers who had ripped open a portal in space and time.

The down-and-out bum had apparently signed on for a research study at the facility along with several others who were picked right off the street. And as he delved into his memories of the fateful night that the "Montauk monster" was unleashed, he became absolutely certain that Nichols had been one of the scientists on hand for the event. Nichols, though, had no idea of what the man was talking about, and at first he took it to be nothing more than the rantings of an unhinged mind.

But many of those rantings would be confirmed when a man named Duncan Cameron sought Nichols's aid in unlocking his own scrambled memories through hypnotic regression. Cameron had also worked at the Montauk facility, and like many of his former colleagues he suffered from a suspiciously specific type of amnesia. While he knew that he had worked at the base, he had no memory of what he'd done there. Several years' worth of clocking in and out on at this job—an entire section of his life—had been wiped clean from his memory.

To make a rather long and complicated story short, Nichols claims that he hypnotized Cameron and discovered the truth about Montauk's manipulation of time and space. Under hypnosis, Cameron stated that he was not originally from our timeline. As a soldier during World War II, he had been part of a crew of test subjects stationed on the deck of the Navy's USS Eldridge when the infamous Philadelphia Experiment was carried out. The Philadelphia Experiment was allegedly an attempt to use powerful magnetic fields to render naval vessels invisible to radar. Supposedly, this had the unanticipated result of warping the space-time around the ship, which made the Eldridge invisible to the naked eye as well and also teleported her from Philadelphia to the coast of Virginia. Cameron somehow jumped ship and ended up in the future, where the Montauk Project retained his services as a psychic.

It all sounds much stranger than anything that the writers of *Stranger Things* have come up with, but that's what Nichols says Cameron said. And as Cameron continued his strange narrative, he confirmed the ramblings of the transient Nichols had encountered at the base, telling Nichols that he was indeed a part of the Montauk Project.

With Cameron's memory restored, Nichols sought to regain his own lost memories as well. These proved to be just as startling, involving as they did visions of a strange device called the "Montauk Chair" that had either been created with technical components from an extraterrestrial civilization or been outright handed over to humans by the ETs. This chair apparently amplified the telepathic ability of anyone who sat in it, and it was through this technological wonder that psychics such as Duncan Cameron were able to open up portals in time and space.

The Arrival of Al Bielek

It was through one of these time portals that another figure central to the Montauk story emerged: a man named Al Bielek. Bielek, who passed away in 2011, was a well-known figure in the world of conspiracy theory and the paranormal. He was a regular fixture on the lecture circuit, and though his written material is rather scant, he logged many hours of oral testimony amounting to—as he himself would always readily admit—some incredibly bizarre claims. Until the day he died, Bielek was adamant that he knew exactly what the future held. In fact, thanks to the folks at Montauk, he had been there to find out firsthand.

Specifically, he said that he traveled to the year 2137, although "traveled" is merely an operative word here. According to Bielek, he stepped through the time portal and the next thing he knew he was waking up in a hospital bed in a high-tech medical center in the distant future. He had apparently been discovered lying out in the open somewhere, unconscious and suffering from some sort of radiation burns acquired during his trip through hyperspace. Medical personnel were now trying to treat his injuries with machines that projected light waves and vibrations through his body. And, you might ask, how did the hospital staff feel about a burned-up time traveler suddenly appearing in their midst? Were they shocked? Baffled? According to Bielek, they weren't actually all that surprised, just interested in interviewing him to learn more about his time period for their historical records.

Bielek's stay in 2137 lasted a little over a month, and then, just about as soon as his radiation burns healed, he mysteriously popped out of that time stream and reemerged even further afield in the year 2749. Here, Bielek claimed, he stayed much longer, about two years, and used the time to learn quite a lot about the world of the mid-28th century.

One of the first things he noticed was how under-populated it seemed. There were no crowds to speak of, and people were relatively scarce everywhere he went. His hosts explained to him that this was deliberate; population controls were actively enforced, and as a result the entire planet had a more or less constant population of just under 300 million people (less than that of the present-day U.S.). This low figure had been determined to be the optimum number of people that the Earth could support and still provide maximum resources for everyone.

In the 21st century the world population has reached seven billion, and for now this massively larger number seems sustainable. In the long term, though, it is unknown whether Earth can continue to provide for this many people—especially if some disaster depletes the planet's already strained resources. According to Bielek, the world of the future did not have this worry.

War was no longer a concern either; since humanity had a constant overabundance at their disposal, there was no fighting over food, water, oil or anything else. Accordingly, there were also no borders. This futuristic Earth had gotten rid of the long-ingrained concept of the nation state for good, creating one seamless planet for all mankind.

This planet was overseen by no president, no emperor, no conventional ruler at all. Humanity had become so fed up with the foibles and petty squabbles of human politicians that they had willingly turned the reins of power over to a "synthetic computer" that now ran the entire world. Bielek learned that this computer had been created 200 years before and was so powerful that it could carry out massive, global-level computations in real time, seamlessly controlling every function of the planet.

While the remote viewers of Project Stargate had foreseen similar advances in artificial intelligence leading to computer systems that could function without human input, their predictions were for a time much closer to our own and on a much smaller scale. According to Bielek, by the 28th century AI will literally rule the world. Fortunately, far from the nightmarish science fiction scenarios of AI taking over and vaporizing humanity, Bielek envisioned a veritable utopia. No one had to work, all of humanity's needs were taken care of, and the world was at peace. There was no need of money—everyone had an allotment of "credits" to purchase whatever manufactured goods they needed—and no one did without. The only true workers were the handful of engineers who knew how the computers worked and remained on standby just in case any repairs or adjustments needed to be made. But for the most part, the world ran itself without any need of human help.

Since humanity was united under the benevolent hegemony of artificial intelligence, there was no need for a standing army. However, the world retained some military capability in the form of massive automated energy weapons—particle beams, lasers and the like—buried in underground silos. Even with peace on Earth, the rest of the universe was an unpredictable place, and the governing computer had decided that it wouldn't be wise to leave the planet completely defenseless. These weapons could be used to repel an alien attack from outer space if the occasion ever happened to present itself.

Al Bielek said that these fantastic visions of the future changed his life forever. And if they're true—who could blame him? Most of us wouldn't have remained anywhere near as calm and mild mannered as Bielek was if such extraordinary things had happened to us. So, should we believe him? Well, whether we believe him or not, as the writers of *Stranger Things* have confirmed, it makes for quite a good story!

Aliens from Outer Space or Travelers from Future Time?

If you're overly familiar with the UFO mythos that has been bandied about for decades and need a plot twist to liven things up, a relatively good one is the concept that these big-headed "space aliens" are actually nothing more than humans from the future. Although it must be admitted that this represents just a small, oft-overlooked subset of UFO theory, the few claims that have been made in this regard are worth taking note of all the same.

The Rendlesham Forest Incident

The Rendlesham Forest Incident, which took place in December of 1980, is actually one of the most famous cases in all of Ufology. It involved U.S. military personnel who were posted at an airbase in Britain, and the case provides not only eyewitness accounts from unusually credible sources but also a rather memorable audio recording that documents their reactions to the UFO in real time.

The part of this story that many tend to miss is that during later hypnotic regression, one of the participants offered up an alternative to the conventional narrative connecting UFOs to ETs. This soldier was firmly convinced that the craft they encountered came not from a distant planet but from our own distant future.

But before we delve into the potential ramifications of this theory, let's just go over the basic background of the Rendlesham Forest Incident. The UFO was first encountered in the early morning hours of December 26, 1980, by members of a security detail who saw a strange illuminated object land between the trees of Rendlesham Forest. Unable to take this invasion of base airspace lying down, the team immediately set off in pursuit.

One of the soldiers in the group, a man named Jim Penniston, later recalled that they found a hovering craft of unknown origin. He was able to make brief physical contact with the UFO, running his hand across its "warm surface", and he also managed to memorize several symbols he observed on its exterior, which later reproduced with pen and paper. Penniston was not sure how long he stood in front of the vehicle, but at some point the UFO made a sudden departure, rising off the ground and rocketing away at a high rate of speed, leaving some very puzzled soldier in its wake.

The experience was so unreal that many of the eyewitnesses, upon waking up the next morning, wondered if the whole thing had been a dream. But when they went back to the woods and investigated the area in question, they knew that they hadn't been imagining things. There were telltale signs of the vehicle's appearance all around them—disturbed soil, burnt grass and broken branches—and all the animals on a nearby farm were making an incredible ruckus, obviously still very spooked by *something*.

The men reported their findings to their superior officer, Lieutenant Colonel Charles Halt, who decided to investigate further. They returned to the site in the still very dark early morning hours of December 28th and began a thorough cataloguing of physical trace evidence, taking soil samples and documenting elevations in radiation. As they worked they noticed a flashing light off in the distance next to an old farmhouse. Suspecting that this was not just some farmer trying to show off his new tractor, they group became quite excited at the prospect of the mystery craft's return.

Moving toward light, they saw to a tripod-shaped vehicle hovering a few feet off the ground. There were no windows, but the craft was covered in lights—it was lit up almost like some kind of elaborate Christmas ornament. Halt claims that the object soon began to drip "something that looked like metal" and then proceeded to defy physics by breaking into "several smaller, white-colored objects" which raced off in all directions.

The airbase commander, Colonel Ted Conrad, reported a separate incident in which his men played a game of cat and mouse with the object. Every time they "came within 50 yards of the ship" it would rise up and move farther out of their reach. This evasiveness makes it seem even stranger that Jim Penniston was able to walk right up and lay his hand on the craft during the initial encounter—and in the end it was Jim Penniston who relayed the strangest news of all when he revealed that the pilots of the mysterious vehicle had given him a message.

Penniston claims that in the days following the encounter, he would wake up in the middle of the night with "visions of ones and zeros running through [his] mind." He came to believe that when he touched the side of the craft that day, it somehow downloaded information directly into his brain. And as the numbers kept repeating in his mind, he felt compelled to let them out. As if on automatic pilot, Penniston grabbed the notebook next to his bed and jotted them all down. It worked. As soon as he transferred the numbers to his notebook, the strange sensation of repeating digits ceased.

Penniston kept the notebook, but he mostly forgot about it for the next few decades. It wasn't until 2010 that he went public with his findings. Contacting computer science experts, he learned that what he had jotted down half-asleep was a complex binary code. Startlingly, these experts also informed him that they could translate the code into English. It read, in part, "Exploration of Humanity—Continuous for Planetary Advancement—Fourth Coordinate Continue—Eyes of Your Eyes—Origin—52.0942532N—Origin Year 8100".

Besides the encoded English message, Penniston's notebook contained other numbers—such as the "Origin" number—that appeared to be coordinates for physical locations. And of course, the intriguing "Origin Year" appears to date the craft to the year 8100. As a result of these findings, Penniston is now convinced that he was given a peaceful message by time travelers from the year 8100 who were conducting an "exploration of humanity".

And the zeroes and ones apparently weren't the whole message. Penniston decided to undergo hypnotic regression to see if he could find out more about his experience, and when the hypnotherapist asked him point-blank why the time travelers had come, he was able to give an immediate answer. He somehow intuitively knew that these future humans were collecting biological material to “heal their world”. In a neat correspondence to a prominent theme in the standard alien-variety UFO mythos, these future humans had hit an evolutionary dead end and were dying out. In order to salvage their degenerating race, they needed to restock their gene pool with good old 20th and century DNA!

Does that sound more than a little farfetched? Probably—but Jim Penniston, Charles Halt, and others continue to stand by their story.

Men in Black—Time Cops on the Beat?

Ah, the menacing Men in Black, the dreadful, dark-clothed strangers who mysteriously show up at the doors of UFO witnesses to dissuade them from coming forward with their accounts. The stories of Men in Black encounters are often every bit as bizarre as the encounters with extraterrestrials that allegedly prompt them. MIB look almost like regular human beings, but something always seems a bit off. Their social interactions are strained and robotic, their movements choppy and awkward. These strange visitors most certainly do not set their hosts at ease.

But even stranger than their mannerisms is the fact that these MIB seem to know everything about any given UFO witness. Not only that, they have been known to visit such witnesses mere minutes after their UFO sighting! In several cases, someone has seen something strange in the sky and then been accosted just moments later by an MIB telling him not to tell anyone else about it. The person has barely had time to register the event himself and hasn't told a soul about it, yet these black-clad men somehow know everything. Who told them? How could they have known so quickly?

According to some theorists, the answer to this question is that the MIB are from the future and are methodically going back in time to contain UFO sightings that occurred in their past. Usually wait a few days after a sighting to harass a witness, but they sometimes seem to cut things a little too close and show up just seconds after the sighting occurred. In one documented case, the MIB even showed up *before* a sighting occurred and ended up intimidating a future UFO witness before he had even seen one in the first place!

It has also been pointed out that the Men in Black seem to be perpetually stuck in the past with their suits, fedoras and vintage Cadillacs. Such accouterments were unremarkable when MIB sightings first began in the late 1940s, but they have long since become conspicuously dated. To some theorists, this indicates an origin outside of our time stream. Any self-respecting time traveler would *try* to fit in to the times and places he visited, but he couldn't be expected to get it quite right. Perhaps, when the MIB first arrived in our era, they picked up a 40s fashion magazine, calibrated their look accordingly, and have simply failed to update their manuals in the decades since.

But even assuming that the Men in Black are time travelers, why would they care about covering up UFO sightings? It's all in their past, right? The explanation is that this theory also posits that the UFOs are actually time machines. If that's the case, it makes perfect sense that future authorities would be worried about them changing the past. It has been speculated that something as subtle as a time traveler stepping on a butterfly in his past could permanently alter his future—a phenomenon often referred to as the "butterfly effect". How much more so, then, a proven UFO sighting? So maybe the Men in Black are time cops desperately trying to preserve their future timeline from destruction by silencing witnesses to vehicles and beings that were never supposed to be here in the first place.

Strange? Scary? You bet it is!

For more on the men in black, I invite you to read my book on this very fascinating subject.

Die Glocke—Die Gift from Die Time Travelers?

Toward the end of World War II, as Allied soldiers were closing in on the Nazi heartland, very few Germans had any hope of victory. The fascist dictator Adolf Hitler was also fairly disillusioned, but until the very end he still behaved as if he had an ace up his sleeve. Even though his cities were being bombed and his armies were being decimated, Hitler didn't place his hopes in just tanks and infantry divisions.

As surviving members of his inner circle would attest, the Nazi tyrant had a tremendous amount of faith in top secret projects to create "wonder weapons". Hitler believed that scientific breakthroughs would enable the construction of powerful new weaponry that would turn the tide of the war. So did the Allies, for that matter—but while the U.S. actually did succeed in developing the first nuclear weapons, Hitler's scientists never got very close to a Nazi A-bomb.

However, they were much more successful in the area of advanced aircraft and rockets. For example, the Germans were able to deploy the world's first jet fighter, the Messerschmitt Me 262, after rushing the prototype into production during the last year of the war. The plane easily outmatched Allied fighters, and if it had been introduced a few years earlier it might have won the Battle of Britain or prevented the D-Day invasion. But this wonder weapon came too late. In the last months of the war, the jets couldn't even get off the ground because all of their runways had been bombed. In the end, the Me 262s captured in their subterranean hangars were just a bonus prize for the conquering American and Russian armies. The victors quickly created their own jet fighters with the help of these Nazi originals, and following the declassification of Project Paperclip—a postwar program in which the U.S. granted amnesty to Nazi scientists who agreed to work on American aerospace projects—this part of the Germans' wartime innovation has become fairly common knowledge.

What remains the stuff of legend is an alleged Nazi R&D program culminating in a device called "Die Glocke"—German for "The Bell", from its shape—which had a primitive antigravity capability and could even warp the fabric of space and time. It must be stressed that everything about Die Glocke is conjecture; there is no solid evidence that the program even existed.

However, several anonymous sources claiming to have been involved in the creation of this rudimentary time machine came forward during the postwar era. They consistently depicted Die Glocke as a solid metal bell 8 feet wide and 12 feet high. Inside were two cylinders filled with a mysterious superconductor called Xerum 525. These cylinders rotated rapidly counterclockwise, generating an incredibly intense gravitational field.

Gravity, as Einstein's theory of relativity teaches us, has a direct effect on time. And the gravity generated by Die Glocke was sufficient to warp space-time in the immediate vicinity. In some instances, the circular "effect zone" of this space-time manipulation extended as far as 660 feet away from the bell itself. The phenomenon caused the device to levitate, but as the Germans could not figure out how to control its flight, they kept it chained to a steel circle on the floor.

This metal ring actually exists: It can still be found at an old Nazi test site, looking like some miniature iron Stonehenge. It is the only physical evidence of the Die Glocke experiments, and skeptics suggest that it was nothing more than the platform for a cooling tower.

But if we are to entertain the possibility that the Germans really did build a flying time machine, we would have to ask, where did they get the idea for such an exotic device? Was this simply the German version of the Manhattan Project, with the country's most brilliant scientists pushed to the limit in order to produce spectacular results? Or, as conspiracy theorists have long speculated, did they have some sort of help? Were they given secrets of advanced technology? And if so—by whom? Many have pointed the finger to some sort of interstellar Molotov–Ribbentrop Pact between the brutal Nazi regime and a group of equally unsavory extraterrestrials.

Others, though have posited an even stranger theory. No prize for guessing what it is: They say that it wasn't visitors from another planet, but visitors from another timeline who dropped this wonder weapon into Hitler's lap. There was certainly a mystical branch of the SS steeped in all manner of myths and legends, and perhaps their esoteric efforts to contact extraplanar entities somehow put them in touch with beings from the future.

Of course, if that's true, it leaves us with an uncomfortable question: Why would the denizens of the future wish to tip the scales in the Nazis' favor? If they were trying to help a group as awful as the Nazis, let's hope they weren't from our future but from some rather abysmal alternate. And with our own timeline so far intact, let's make sure that the only thing that ever goosesteps again is a goose!

Alleged Time Travelers and Other Strange Correspondence

Finding someone like Al Bielek, who actually claimed to be a time traveler, used to be extremely rare. But nowadays it seems like new claims are popping up on social media every single day. There are countless would-be time travelers trolling YouTube and Facebook with tantalizing visions of the future. The chrononuts (pun fully intended) are coming out of the woodwork, but there's no telling whether any of their bizarre stories are true. There is no real evidence either way, so the veracity of these tales has to be evaluated by those who hear them. In this chapter, we have listed a litany of some of the most popular claims of alleged time travelers so that you can decide for yourself.

The Diary of Paul Dienach

The story of Paul Amadeus Dienach's forays into the future sounds strangely similar to Al Bielek's account. Both men supposedly woke up in a hospital bed in the distant future, and both encountered many of the same technologies, concepts, and situations. Either the two exchanged notes somewhere along the line—or they really did separately experience the same phenomenon and the same general future that awaits us all.

Dienach was a mild-mannered teacher in early 20th-century Switzerland before he became an accidental time traveler. In 1921 he came down with a bad case of encephalitis lethargica and was hospitalized in Geneva. Doctors watched helplessly as his brain began to swell and he fell into a coma. The outlook seemed bleak, and nearly all hope was lost. But even as his body became comatose, Dienach himself was waking up. Not in a Swiss hospital, though, and not in 1921.

The next thing he knew, he was in 3906—and not only that, he was no longer Paul Dienach. He found himself inside the body of a man named Andrew Northman. Dienach was naturally terrified, but he took some consolation from the fact that those who greeted him in 3906 seemed to understand exactly what had happened. After he explained his predicament, he was taken to be interviewed by a panel of experts who deduced that he had just gone through a completely spontaneous "temporal slip".

But although these worthies knew enough to understand and accept this odd event, they had no idea how to send Dienach back. So, determined to make the best of his time in the future, he began learning as much as he could. He also provided eager historians with intimate details of life in the 1920s, helping them to clarify long-held misconceptions.

Dienach received many startling revelations about what the future held for humanity. Significant for us today, he was told that acts of terror would become common by the early 2000s and lead to decades of intermittent war in a severely divided world—one of the plainer predictions of 9/11 and its aftermath from any prophet. In a development sure to horrify libertarians everywhere, the scourge of terror and anarchy would finally be eliminated by a one-world government wielding global police powers. With no place to hide and no chance of safe haven anywhere on the planet, terrorist cells quickly died out and an authoritarian super-state ushered in an era of world peace.

And from what Dienach could gather, the people of 3906 truly had adopted a gentle, almost childlike and entirely peaceful way of life. The suspicions of yesteryear had passed out of society, and everyone seemed to embrace each other as brothers and sister.

The advent of this universal peace had allowed a period of intense learning that produced several notable technological breakthroughs. In the 22nd century, one of the greatest scientists the world had ever known, a man named Andreas Nortrom, had discovered how to manipulate gravity. This led to the creation of a “field gate” which allowed people to walk through gravitational gateways and emerge a vast distance away on the other side. These shortcuts even linked Earth to Mars, completely negating the need even for interplanetary spaceflight and leading to rapid colonization of the Red Planet. By 2204, Mars had huge, self-sustained human cities spanning its surface.

But even with such advanced technology, mankind could still be caught completely off guard by the unexpected, unknown quantities of the universe. In 2234, explorers in the Martian desert accidentally released super-virus that had been lying dormant for untold eons. This alien virus wreaked havoc on unprepared human immune systems and quickly decimating the Martian population. Mars was quarantined, the Martian field gates were shut down, and no one was allowed to travel to or from the Red Planet lest the virus be brought to Earth. The plague eventually ran its course, but the Martian colonies never recovered from its devastating death toll.

Soon after this calamity, scientists working on the field gate technology used it to discover an intelligent alien civilization. These beings had thought they were alone in the universe, and they were fairly shocked when a curious humanity came ringing their interstellar doorbell, but they seem to have been friendly enough.

Toward the end of the 23rd century, advances in genetic manipulation gave rise to widespread transhumanism. People were able to map their own genomes, directly regulate gene expression, and customize their physical forms however they wished. It was the ultimate fulfillment of the 21st century concept of the designer baby, and these newly designed adults were classified as "*Homo novus*"—which of course means "new humans".

Dienach ended up living in the future for about a year before fading out just as spontaneously as he'd arrived and opening his eyes to find himself back in a hospital bed in Switzerland in 1921. It would be easy to say that his experiences were no more than the fever dreams of encephalitis lethargica. But Dienach would remain convinced for the rest of his life that what he experienced was no dream—and incredibly, he would never say a word about what had transpired to anyone else. He simply moved on with his life as a teacher as if nothing at all out of the ordinary had happened in that Geneva hospital.

The only reason we know the story is because Dienach wrote it all down in a diary which he bequeathed to a young man who had been one of his students. As he lay on his deathbed, slipping out of this life for a second and final time, Dienach instructed his former pupil to read the diary and then destroy it. After Dienach passed on and the man went through the book, he was amazed at what he found. At first he tried to rationalize the strange tale as an unpublished novel, but the way it was written clearly indicated that it was a first-hand account. And besides, if it were just a novel, why the cryptic admonition to destroy it?

In the end, Dienach's alumnus did not heed his deathbed dictate. He went on to publicize the narrative for posterity, and now we can all examine this odd tale on our own and decide for ourselves whether it contains any kernel of truth. Perhaps one day someone will find some hidden meaning and come to a new understanding of just what Dienach experienced. But as it stands, Paul Dienach's mind-bending journey remains a true mystery in the annals of space and time.

John Titor Saves the World

John Titor went viral before "viral" even existed, all the way back in the early 2000s. His sole claim to fame was sporadically posting messages on an internet forum with wild claims of being from the year 2036. Amazingly enough, this gained him a substantial cult following, which seems to be a clear indication either that he was telling the truth—or that he had an utterly fantastic sense of plot development. Because the story of John Titor—whether you categorize it as science fiction or biography—has more than enough drama for a bestselling novel or a Hollywood screenplay.

It begins mundanely enough—insofar as a time travel story can be mundane—with Titor being sent on a military mission to 1975 to pick up an old IBM computer. His superiors needed this particular computer because it had a completely unique ability to rewrite UNIX code. It seems that the computers of 2036, which still relied on UNIX, were headed for a major glitch in the next couple of years unless their code was reset.

Now, this unique IBM sounds like an interesting MacGuffin for a sci-fi story. The only thing is, it actually existed—and John Titor had no business knowing anything about it. As the chatter about Titor's claims grew, stunned representatives from IBM felt compelled to weigh in on the issue and confirm that this particular model of computer did indeed have the capabilities that Titor had mentioned. However, that information had been a closely guarded trade secret at Big Blue. Only a few top engineers had been privy to it, and they were mystified—not to say alarmed and outraged—at how it had finally leaked to the public.

IBM's reaction proved that Titor wasn't a complete fantasist. He might be a time traveler just like he said he was—or he might be an unidentified IBM insider willing to risk his pension just to tell a good story. Titor himself stated that his grandfather actually had been an IBM employee back in 1975, and that this personal connection was part of the reason he was picked for the assignment—his superiors apparently believed that it might help facilitate the heist.

But Titor hadn't come back in time just to be a thief. He also wanted to warn the world that America would become increasingly polarized and divided. On his timeline, this discord led to an outright civil war which only ended when Russia interceded on behalf of one of the belligerents with limited nuclear strikes. Russia's American allies prevailed, but at a terrible cost. The nukes had obliterated most of the major urban centers, leaving the winning faction to literally climb back out of the rubble.

As grim as Titor's own future was, however, he always stressed that it was just one possible future, and that it could be averted if people took the correct actions soon enough. He explained that in his 2036, the many-worlds theory of quantum mechanics had been proven correct. This would mean that there are an infinite number of possible universes filling up an infinite number of dimensions in time and space. Everything and anything could be—and is—happening somewhere in the multiverse at any given time. As Titor stated in his posts, the fact that something had happened in the timeline he came from didn't necessarily mean it would happen in the timeline his audience was headed for.

Of course, if John Titor was a fraud, this theory would also provide a convenient escape hatch. If all of his predictions about the future failed, he could always say, "Well, of course that didn't happen here. You guys are on a different timeline!"

Titor also used the idea of parallel universes as the ultimate solution to the age-old grandfather paradox. Many have argued that the paradox makes time travel impossible, because if for example, someone went back in time and murdered his own grandfather, the time traveler's father, and subsequently the time traveler himself, would never be born. Therein lies the ungainly paradox: If the time traveler was never born, how would he be able to travel back in time to kill his grandfather in the first place?

But according to Titor, the many-worlds theory neatly explains how this scenario would play out. If someone was actually crazy enough to go back in time to kill his grandfather (sorry, Gramps!), the murder would immediately create a brand-new timeline. The original timeline that the time traveler came from would remain intact and unaltered. There would now be a parallel timeline/universe in which the time traveler's family line ended with his grandfather. But back in the time traveler's native timeline, he would still exist, his father would still exist, and his grandfather would never have been killed. So Titor was right about at least one thing—the many-worlds theory really does solve the grandfather paradox.

He also seems to have been right about at least one aspect of time machine design. He claimed that his own time machine ran on dual mini black holes operating on principles that Stephen Hawking would eventually champion—and several years later the great physicist came out in favor of just such a theory. As many experts in many different fields have commented, whoever was behind the Titor posts was extremely knowledgeable, sometimes uncannily so, about a wide variety of complex disciplines.

So was John Titor a time traveler, a complete fraud, or just a really astute and prescient kind of guy? So far, nobody else has been astute enough to figure that out for sure!

Michael Phillips's Message from the Future

Depending on who you talk to, the strange story of Michael Phillips's alleged adventures in time travel either corroborates John Titor's tale or denigrates it by exposing yet another hoaxer attempting to seize hold of the public's imagination. You see, when Phillips first came forward in 2018, he not only claimed to be from the future, he claimed to be a personal acquaintance of the internet time traveling legend John Titor.

And like Titor, Phillips has a whole bag of bad prophecies for very near future. Among them, he insists that there is a high probability that World War III will be initiated by 2020, most likely by a North Korean nuclear strike on Hawaii. Now, despite President Trump's recent efforts to reduce tensions with North

Korea, that's still entirely possible. On the other hand, it really doesn't take a time traveler to tell us that.

However, Phillips goes into further detail. He claims that after North Korea lobs a nuke at Hawaii, the U.S responds within minutes, taking out Kim Jung Un, his military and most of North Korea with its own nuclear arsenal. Although the U.S. is the obvious victor in this "quick and brutal" exchange, it triggers a third world war with Russia and China moving against the United States and the United Kingdom. Fortunately, cooler heads prevail during this conflict and the war between the Russia/China axis and the U.S./British alliance does not go nuclear. Conventional attacks still cause a tremendous loss of life on all sides, but after three years World War III ends with a truce and the world settles back to as close to normal as it can after so much carnage.

Phillips also predicts that President Trump will be elected to a second term and then attempt to do away with term limits and gain a third term as well. But he is impeached before he can succeed, and the 2024 presidential election becomes a contest between former talk show host Oprah Winfrey and a man named Michael Macintosh. After a hard-fought campaign, Macintosh defeats Oprah and goes on to become the 46th President of the United States. His leadership reinvigorates the country and sparks a number of new initiatives.

In the area of space exploration, this newfound vitality seems to be concentrated in the private sector. NASA falls increasingly behind companies headed by tech entrepreneurs who have grown tired of the old space agency's never-ending red tape. Taking matters into their own hands, these men use their money and technical knowhow to finally make routine manned space travel a reality. Elon Musk successfully lands a manned mission on Mars.

But will the increasingly irascible Musk really hang on that long? Who the heck is Michael Macintosh? Are these just the random ramblings of a lunatic? Well, whatever the answers to the first two questions are, the answer to the last is almost certainly no. Even if he's not a time traveler, the tales that Michael Phillips weaves seem to be fairly insightful musings about potential future trends.

Alexander Smith
the Time Traveling Secret Agent

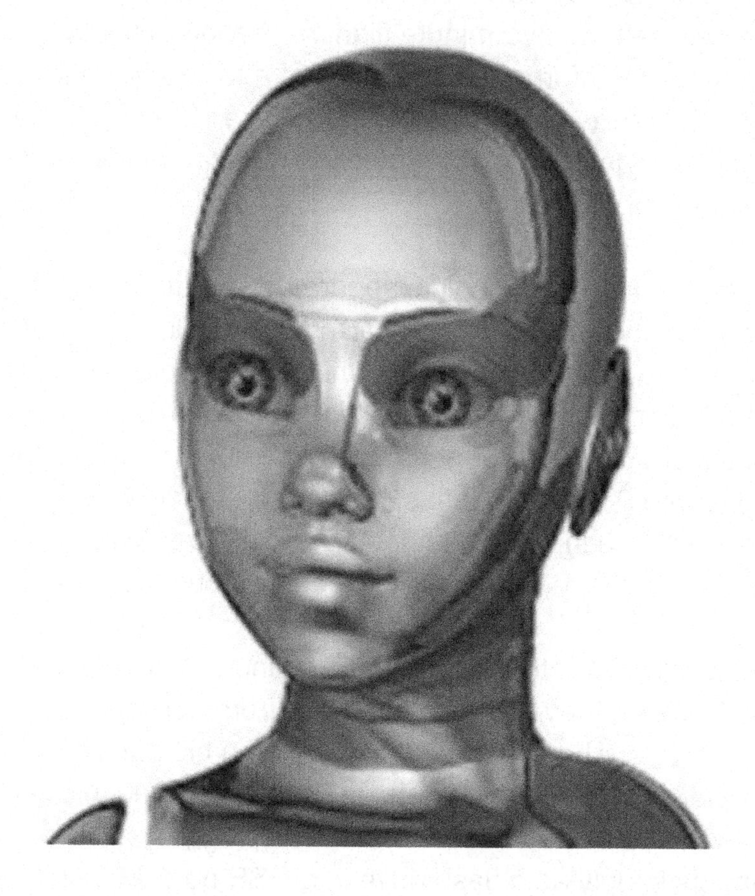

Alexander Smith is one of the most recent alleged time travelers to make the rounds on YouTube. Thought by most to be a hoaxer—and a rather bad one at that—Smith is peddling a narrative that back in 1981, the CIA sent him on an experimental trip through time to the year 2118.

Smith was a military veteran with previous links to the agency, but his selection for the project seemed to be completely random. Agents dressed all in black (Men in Black?) arrived at his door and ordered him to drop everything and come with them. The men then led him to their car and blindfolded him before starting the engine and taking him for a ride. When the car eventually stopped and Smith was taken outside, he could hear the blades of a nearby helicopter. He was led into the chopper, and after a five-minute flight his handlers finally took off the blindfold and informed that he was at a top-secret military installation. They led him from the landing pad down several flights of stairs and a long hallway, then directed him to enter a room on his right.

Inside was an immense cubical apparatus sprouting a multitude of gauges and wires. There were also strange slot-like openings in its front side. As Smith stared at the strange contraption, a man in a lab coat bluntly informed him, "This is a time machine." The scientist and his colleagues went on to explain that they wanted to use Smith as a test subject for the device—and that the risks included injury, death, and being forever lost in time. For whatever reason, Smith readily agreed to be their guinea pig.

The scientists promptly placed him in a kind of "tin suit" and helmet, in order, they said, to shield him from dangerous radiation levels. They instructed him to lie on his back on a sort of stretcher, which was then hoisted up and inserted into one of the slots on the time machine. Smith was plugged into the machine as snugly as a flash drive in a USB port. At first it was completely dark, but after a moment he began to see repetitive flashes of light flickering through the contraption. Then, it seems, he temporarily lost consciousness.

The next thing he knew he was waking up in a hospital bed (seemingly a common theme with time travel). But this hospital was unlike anything he had seen before. In front of him he saw what looked like a large sheet of glass literally floating in front of the wall. When he looked over to his left, he saw a glass tabletop which was also seemed to be suspended in midair.

A nurse soon walked into the room and explained that Smith had been admitted to the hospital after being found lying comatose right in the middle of a road. He started to tell her his story, but she cut him off by asking when it had taken place. When Smith gave the date in 1981, the nurse stared at him incredulously before informing him, “Sir, it’s 2118.”

Smith was astonished, but he realized that he couldn’t argue about it without looking like he was completely insane. When the nurse left, he reached for what looked like a TV remote and hit the power button. The sheet of glass floating over the wall sprang to life, revealing its purpose as a TV screen. Smith didn’t recognize any of the programs, but as he channel-surfed, he eventually stumbled upon some sort of news program. The date in the bottom corner read November 17th, 2118.

Beginning to panic, Smith turned off the television and got up. The staff hadn’t bothered to put him in a hospital gown—he was still wearing the same clothes he’d been wearing in 1981—so he simply walked out of the room and made a beeline for the nearest elevator. No one stopped him.

When the elevator doors opened on first-floor lobby, Smith saw a roomful of people all dressed in the same exact clothing, a pair of white pants and a white long-sleeved shirt. His own attire obviously stood out, and he received quite a few bewildered looks, but he ignored them and walked outside to the street.

He was greeted by a large sign emblazoned with the enigmatic words “District 508 of the Yavis Empire”. Where was he—and just what was the Yavis Empire? In complete shock, Smith started to stumble wildly through the bizarre futuristic metropolis he found himself lost in.

Even in the midst of his panic, Smith was intrigued to see that there were no cars on the streets, just throngs of pedestrians and bicyclists. It didn't take him long to figure out where the motorized vehicles were: He looked up to find them whizzing above his head. This future, at least, lived up to the hoary sci-fi trope of the flying car. The city still seemed to be suffering from heavy rush hour traffic, but since it had been moved several miles into the air, the streets were completely free for foot traffic. Smith saw all kinds of people from all walks of life traversing these streets.

He also saw entities that were apparently robots. These robots were nearly indistinguishable from people from the waist up, but they didn't have legs. They were basically anthropomorphic torsos with a head and arms, and just like the glass tabletop in the hospital, they floated effortlessly a few feet above the pavement as they intermingled with their human contemporaries.

Reasoning that a robot might be harder to faze than one of his fellow men, Smith approached one and got straight to the point: He asked where he could find a time machine. Without batting an electronic eyelash, the robot replied that he needed to go to a time travel agency. (Well, *obviously*!) The helpful robot then handed him a thin piece of glass, something akin to a tablet. The screen showed a map with his current position and the route to the nearest time travel agency.

When he got there, Smith marched up to the main desk—which was "manned" by another robot—and asked to be sent to 1981. The robot didn't question him; it simply spouted off the price for the trip. Reflexively reaching for his wallet, Smith found the thick wad of cash that the CIA had given him. He had a sinking feeling that it wasn't legal tender in the Yavis Empire, but he also had nothing to lose, so he hesitantly laid the money down in front of the robot to see what would happen. To his relief, the robot simply took the archaic currency, converted it according to some intertemporal exchange rate, and handed back a ticket and some change.

Smith was then led to a “bright blue, shiny machine”. He sat down inside it, and after a few minutes he lost consciousness once again. The next thing he knew he was waking up on the streets of a rough section of Los Angeles. He saw several homeless people nearby, but he wasn’t sure if they had seen his astounding arrival. At any rate, he asked them what year it was, and after some funny looks they told him that he was indeed back in 1981.

Smith’s story is certainly an interesting one. But is there any truth to it? What do people generally believe about this incredible claim? The odd tale has gotten a lot of airplay on YouTube, and several articles have made the rounds—and the reviews are mixed. It seems that those who want to believe it will do so, and those who don’t—won’t. So, I’ll let you be the judge.

Andrew Basiago and Project Pegasus

Andrew Basiago has long filled the airwaves of the internet with tales of clandestine government programs, time travel, and apocalyptic predictions of the future. Basiago claims that back in the 1970s, he was part of a secret military program called Project Pegasus which was responsible for astonishing advances in several technical fields. These supposedly included not only time travel, but also highly efficient interstellar teleportation that could send a man instantly to any point in the universe.

Well, before you put on your tinfoil hat in the face of such grandiose claims, let's at least see what Basiago has to say.

Basiago asserts that he was selected for Project Pegasus due to the fact that he had been "psychically gifted" since childhood. How the military received word of said psychic ability is not exactly clear, but Basiago claims that his father had previously worked as an engineer on several other clandestine projects. He thus already had some degree of familiarity with the work being conducted, and he wasn't completely shocked by the concepts involved.

Soon after Basiago was brought on board he got an up-close-and-personal view of the "jump portals" Project Pegasus used for both time travel and teleportation. They consisted of two parentheses-shaped booms that were 8 feet tall and spaced 10 feet apart. The system was controlled by banks of computers. When the apparatus was switched on, tremendous energy flowed through it to create a "vortal tunnel" that bent time and space. Pegasus personnel could simply walk through this tunnel to other locations and times.

Basiago's first trip was a dry run that just took him to a prearranged location in present-day New Mexico. His next, however, took him to another time and place altogether—back to the 1860s to meet Abraham Lincoln and hear the Gettysburg Address. This was apparently a kind of fact-finding tour to verify certain historical details for the record.

Shortly after this stint in the past, Basiago was sent to the future, to the year 2045 and a high-tech city full of skyscrapers made of emerald and tungsten steel. Meeting up with a prearranged contact, he was given a collection of microfilm containing information on all the major historical events to date.

Wait, microfilm? In 2045? Why wouldn't Basiago's futuristic contact haven given him the data on some more futuristic medium, like a flash drive or an SD card? Well, you have to remember that Basiago was coming from the 1970s. If he'd been handed a flash drive there would have been nowhere to plug it in when he got back. Same thing for a DVD. So, unless he wanted to hand Basiago a few boxes of dead-tree documents, his contact pretty much had to use microfilm to convey the information back to the pre-digital era. That's not to say that Basiago's story as a whole is true, false, or anything in between—but this part actually makes a lot more sense than most people seem to realize.

The next part? Not so much. Basiago has also made the beyond-sensational claim that President Barack Obama was a member of a Project Pegasus team sent to explore Mars in the 1980s. Shortly after the 2008 election, Basiago suddenly came out of the woodwork to allege that Obama, then going by the name of Barry Soetero, had teleported to the Red Planet when he was only 19 years old. Bizarrely, the claim gained enough traction that the President actually felt compelled to respond with a formal denial. And while it's common enough now for the White House to get down and dirty with internet innuendo of all kinds, firing off tweet storms like there's no tomorrow, back in the days of the Obama administration, such a response was pretty much unprecedented.

Well, the world just seems to keep on getting stranger by the day, doesn't it? And the latest word from the Basiago camp is that Basiago is now going to run for president himself! You just can't make this stuff up. This time-traveling renaissance man has already begun his campaign for the presidency, and he says that his contacts from the future have assured him of a win, if not in this election then most certainly in the next. Will President Trump be bested by a time-traveling progressive in 2020? I suppose stranger things have happened.

Current Thoughts and Theories on Time Travel

The concept of time travel has been around just about as long as the concept of time itself. It seems that as soon as man realized that he was trapped inside a finite timeline, all he wanted to do was break out of it. But for the most part these schemes have just been mental flights of fancy, good for science fiction or at most very general speculative theorizing.

No one really believed that time travel might actually be possible—that is, until the discovery of a little something called quantum mechanics. Unlike classical physics, which had a defined set of principles leading to predictable outcomes, quantum mechanics leaves room for much more uncertainty. In fact, one of the fundamental tenants of quantum mechanics is called the "uncertainty principle". Quantum mechanics adds grey areas to the laws of physics, and some former constants now seem not quite so constant after all.

The progression of time is one of these. Albert Einstein's theory of relativity reveals that time, rather than running in a straight line, meanders like a river. The pull of gravity has a direct effect on the quite literal "time stream" that our entire reality rests upon. All of the stars and planets in the universe are basically boulders in the unseen waters of time, and time reacts to their gravitational forces.

Continuing our water analogy, just consider the differing effects a large boat and a small boat have on the water around them. The different sizes of these boats cause the water to ripple around them differently. Einstein discovered that the same is true with time and gravity. The time flowing around the giant planet

Jupiter, for instance, would be slightly different than the time circulating around Earth, due to Jupiter's greater gravitational pull.

Einstein also discovered that time changes the faster you go. For example, if you were on a spaceship traveling at the speed of light, time would slow to a crawl—while back on Earth several hundred years might have gone by. This is phenomenon is called time dilation, and it has been conclusively proven by atomic clocks placed in high-altitude planes, as well as through the GPS satellite network.

Now it is fairly common knowledge that time is not the unchangeable bulwark that we used to imagine. Time can quite literally change, and equipped with this knowledge, many scientists and scholars are hard at work breaking through the final barriers.

Stephen Hawking and the Chronological Protection Conjecture

Stephen Hawking passed away in 2017 without ever building a time machine, but his theories are so intertwined with the subject that he simply has to be mentioned. It was Hawking, after all who first proposed that "singularities", such as those that reside in the depths of black holes, were a permanent fixture of time and space. And it was none other than the infamous John Titor who claimed that his time machine was basically built upon Hawking's theory—it utilized micro-singularities, or in other words micro black holes.

Hawking himself, however, probably would have been skeptical of this claim. In his mind, although time travel to the future was certainly possible due to the proven effects of time dilation, traveling backwards into the past was simply not in the cards. Part of the reason for this belief was a matter of simple common sense: Hawking figured that the fact that we are not being bombarded with time travelers from the future means there aren't any. To put this theory to the test, he once publicly invited any and all time travelers to attend a party he was going to throw at Cambridge University. None showed up, so Hawking concluded that he had either proved his point—or had just been viciously snubbed by the time travel community.

He accordingly challenged his fellow physicists to come up with a more formal proof of the impossibility of time travel to the past. Hawking jokingly referred to it as the Chronology Protection Conjecture and claimed that it was needed to make "history safe for historians". But jokes aside, this launched a serious effort to solve the problem—and as much as seasoned scientists around the world racked their brains to find a way to make time travel obsolete, they just couldn't do it. If anything, after all their efforts, time travel actually seemed more feasible than before.

Hawking was eventually forced to make the grudging admission, "Time travel may be possible, but it is not practical."

Working Your Way through Wormholes

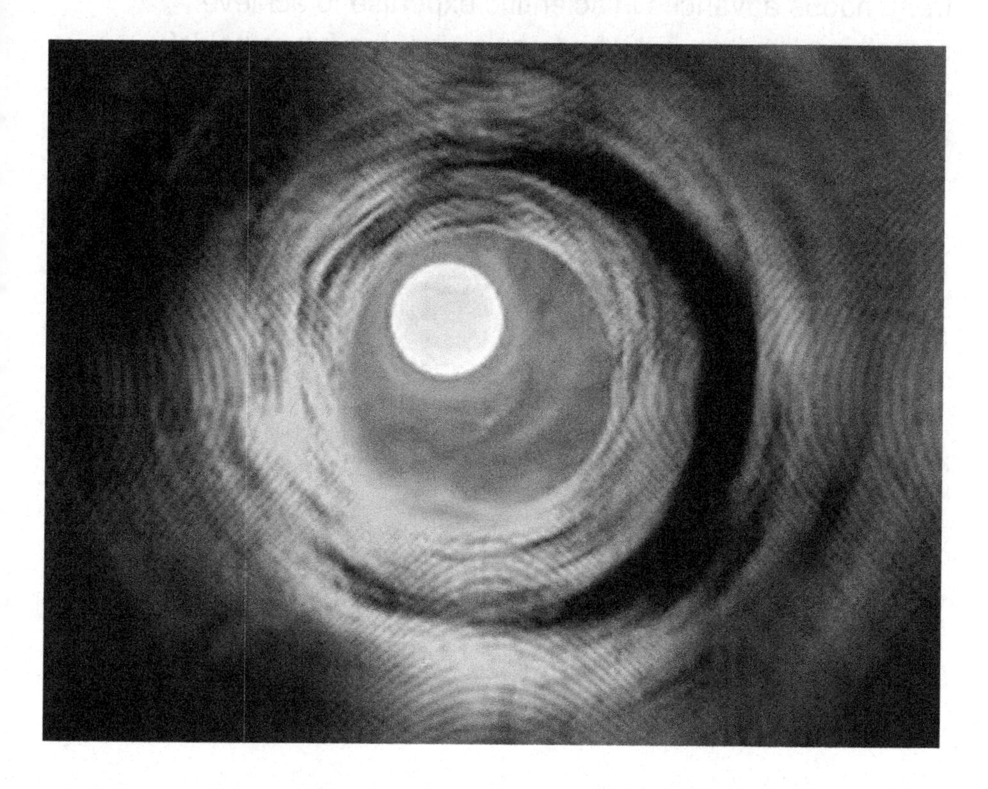

Practical or not, many physicists believe that the best way to travel through time might be to use something called a "wormhole". Also known as "Einstein-Rosen bridges", wormholes have not yet been proven to exist, but all the math seems to indicate that they should. Wormholes, while often thought of as holes in the fabric of space and time, may be better described as tunnels connecting two different points of space-time together.

If a spacecraft could be safely sent through one, it would thus come out the other end in another place and another time. However, wormholes are predicted to be nearly microscopic, so unless you can shrink your spaceship down to the size of a dot, you might be out of luck. Or you might not: Some scientists are hopeful that there may be some way to expand these micro-portals into larger openings, possibly with some exotic energy source currently beyond our understanding. It would take tremendous advances in scientific expertise to achieve something like this, but who knows what the future holds?

The Large Hadron Collider and the Fabric of Space and Time

Nestled underneath the border of France and Switzerland, the Large Hadron Collider is the world's biggest particle accelerator. This accelerator was built to examine the building blocks of the universe by blasting them apart. Particles are propelled at tremendous speed along the massive stretch of the accelerator before colliding into each other. The ensuing explosion and its components are then studied intensively. This meticulous work has already improved our understanding of how the universe works, but what does it mean for time travel?

According to some who have worked with the LHC, it could mean everything. This is because the collider is helping us to understand one of the most enigmatic elements of the universe: dark matter. Some think that harnessing this mysterious substance could literally open up the fabric of space and time. Furthermore, according to LHC insiders, a rudimentary form of time travel has already been witnessed. Some particles seem to return to the beginning of the tunnel before they have left in the first place. This anomaly has apparently occurred during several trial runs.

And although sending microscopic particles backwards in time may not be quite as impressive as sending human beings back in time, some believe that this could be just the beginning. Messages could soon be encoded into particles and sent to recipients in the past, and who knows—one day maybe people could be sent as well.

Ronald Mallet and Time Travel by Laser Light

Ronald Mallet has been obsessed with the idea of traveling back in time since he was 10 years old. Many children his age develop fanciful urges for fantastic feats, but the impetus for Ronald's interest was not a flight of fancy—it was his father's untimely death. Mallet Sr. was only 33 when his heart gave out on him, robbing young Ronald of his beloved father. Ronald knew that he couldn't bring his dad back to life, but after reading a comic book based upon the H.G. Wells classic *The Time Machine*, he began to consider the possibility of going back in time to save him. As touching as this is, you'd expect that Ronald would have grown out of this obsession eventually. But the thing is—he didn't.

Ronald Mallet is now in his early 70s and as determined as ever to go back in time and have a chat with his late father. He'd like to tell him to quit smoking and eat a little better so he never has the heart attack that killed him at such a young age. Mallet has let this desire drive him his whole life, and his work as a theoretical physicist has now made his old dream seem close to becoming reality. Because Mallet now believes that he has found the secret to unlocking time travel.

He has proposed that bending powerful beams of laser light into circles would create “frame dragging” in the gravitational field, eventually leading to “closed time like curves”. These curves, Mallet claims, would allow travel back to the point that the lasers were first flipped on. Of course, he realizes that even if his theory right, it still won’t let him visit his dad. But if it means opening up some form of time travel for future generations, Mallet believes his career will have been worth it.

Just A Matter of Time

As far as we know, human beings are the only life forms that have a concept of time. While the chimpanzee is permanently stuck in the present, we humans frequently dwell on the past and worry about the future. So this rather unique quality of the human brain allows us to time travel—mentally, at least—whenever we like. Yes, it's true—in that sense, every single person is a time traveler!

It is believed that humans developed the notion of time as an evolutionary survival mechanism. The ability to plan ahead presented a great advantage for early humans in an uncertain world, and it has been our obsession ever since.

Ever since our ancestors sparked the first fire and carved the first rock, we have sought to manipulate our environment to our advantage. The caveman couldn't resist scraping at the walls of his cave any more than modern physicists can resist pushing back against the barrier of time. So, keep your eyes peeled and mark your calendars. Perhaps the next major breakthrough is right around the corner, because it really is—just a matter of time. Thank you for reading.

Further Reading and Reference

Now that you have read the book, check out these other great sources of time travel trivia. You will find extra details about the narratives we've already explored and lots more besides. If you enjoyed what you read here, you will love these resources as well.

***Physics of the Impossible: A Scientific Exploration into the World of Phasers, Force Fields, Teleportation, and Time Travel*. Michio Kaku**
Michio Kaku is not only an expert in the field of physics; he is also a great communicator, able to simplify and explain complicated subjects in an entertaining manner. This book proves it. Even if you hate science and theorizing, Kaku livens things up with so many pop culture references and humorous analogies you will still get a kick out of this book.

He covers everything from time travel and wormholes to parallel universes, cosmic strings, and dark matter. As farfetched as some of the current theories in physics may sound, we have to remind ourselves that that the meaning of the word "impossible" is forever open to our own personal interpretations.

***Secret History: Conspiracies from Ancient Aliens to the New World Order*. Nick Redfern**
Nick Redfern is a true veteran in the world of the mysterious. Although this book's main focus is not time travel it offers many interesting asides on the subject. From strange temporal happenings to encounters with the Men in Black to highlights of the Montauk Project, the author of this paranormal tour de force leaves no stone unturned.

***The Truth behind Men in Black*. Jenny Randles**
Randles always has an interesting perspective on—well, just about anything—and this is especially true when it comes to the Men in Black! Randles has studied the concept for decades, and in this book she provides us with almost uncanny insights into the phenomenon. While the whole truth may never be known, Randles at least gives us an excellent starting point to begin to unravel the mystery.

***Above Top Secret: Uncover the Mysteries of the Digital Age*. Jim Mars**
This book has a lot of interesting information, but it's the chapter Mars devoted to the internet legend John Titor that is the most fascinating. Titor truly has been one of the greatest mysteries of the digital age, and Mars tried his best to get to the bottom of it. Sadly, he passed away before fully solving the Titor case, but his research will live on.

***The Mammoth Encyclopedia of Extraterrestrial Encounters*. Ronald D. Story**
This is an anthology collection with a whole lot of information. Just about every case of ET contact is covered in this book. But besides aliens, this compendium also has a wealth of information about time travel and its potential implications. This book is great to have on hand as a reference.

***Time Traveler: A Scientist's Personal Mission to Make Time Travel a Reality*. Ronald Mallet**
In this rather touching narrative, Ronald Mallet relates how his lifelong longing to go back in time to meet up with his deceased father led him to become a physicist studying concepts of time travel. Besides the personal anecdotes, there is a wealth of solid information regarding the use of lasers to warp time. Mallet makes quite an interesting case for time travel.

Conspiracies and Secret Societies: The Complete Dossier.
Brad Steiger
The late, great Brad Steiger knew how to compile a good anthology, and he wrote a lot of them during his illustrious career. But out of them all, this truly stands out.

Also by Conrad Bauer

VOL 2
THE WORLD'S
STRANGEST FORGOTTEN
CONSPIRACY
THEORIES
CONRAD BAUER

The World's Strangest
FORGOTTEN
CONSPIRACY
THEORIES
CONRAD BAUER

Made in the USA
Las Vegas, NV
01 November 2021